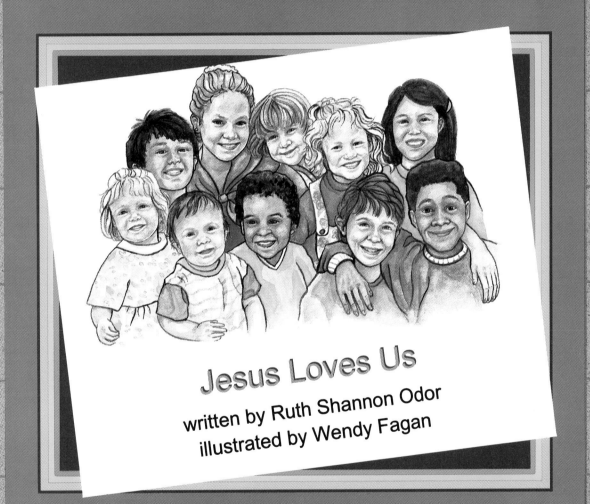

Jesus Loves Us

written by Ruth Shannon Odor

illustrated by Wendy Fagan

The Standard Publishing Company, Cincinnati, Ohio
A division of Standex International Corporation
©1992 by The Standard Publishing Company
All rights reserved.
Printed in the United States of America
99 98 97 96 95 94 93 92   5 4 3 2 1
Library of Congress Catalog Card Number 91-67211
ISBN 0-87403-934-7

All day men, women, boys, and girls had sat and stood on the hillside.
They had come to see Jesus.
Some had come for Jesus to make them well.
"It is late, and the people are hungry," said Jesus' helpers.

Jesus looked at the tired, hungry people.
He felt sorry for them.
Do you know what He did?

TURN THE PAGE ▶▶▶

AND SEE

One little boy had brought his lunch.
It was only five loaves of bread and two fish.
Jesus took the food and thanked God for it.
He told the disciples to give the fish and bread
    to the hungry people.
Suddenly there was more than enough for
    everyone to eat!
Jesus fed the people because He loved them.

O ne day people brought a man to Jesus.
The man could not hear.
He could not hear the song of the birds or the
   wind in the trees or the laughing of
   children.
And he could hardly talk.
Do you know what Jesus did?

TURN THE PAGE ▸▸▸

AND SEE

Jesus took the man away from the crowd.
He touched the man's ears and his tongue.
"Be opened," He said.
Suddenly the man could hear!
He could talk so everyone could understand!
How happy he was!
Jesus loved the man who could not hear.

O ne day a man named Jairus came to Jesus.
He said, "My daughter is very sick. You can
   make her well."
Do you know what Jesus did?

TURN THE PAGE ▸▸▸

AND SEE

Jesus went with Jairus to his house.
The girl was dead.
Jesus took her by the hand.
He said, "Little girl, get up."
The girl opened her eyes. She sat up.
Jesus had made the little girl live again.
Jesus loved the girl and her mother and father.

O ne day another man came to Jesus.
He said, "My little boy is sick. Please come
    and make him well again."
Jesus said, "Go back home. Your son is well."
Do you know what the man found at home?

TURN THE PAGE ▶▶▶

AND SEE

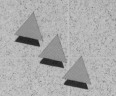

The little boy was well!
The man asked, "When did he get well?"
"Yesterday, about one o'clock," some people said.
The man knew that that was the very minute when Jesus had said the boy would be made well.
Jesus had made the little boy well!
Jesus loved the little boy and his family.

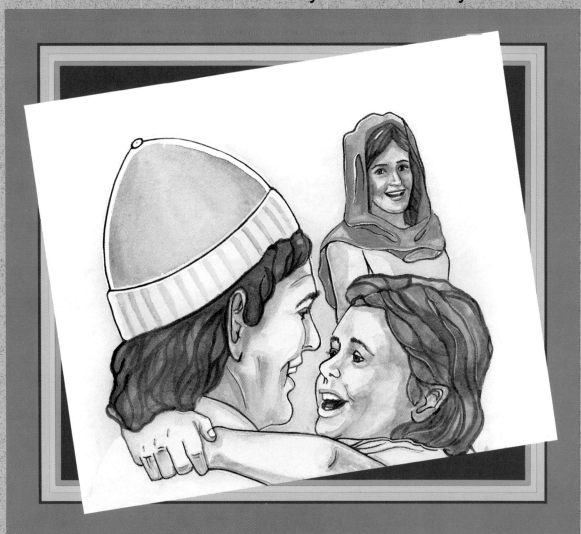

our friends felt sorry for their sick friend.
No one could make him well.
The four friends took him to Jesus.
Many people were in the house with Jesus.
The man's friends let him down through the
    roof.
Do you know what Jesus did?

TURN THE PAGE ▶▶▶

Jesus told the sick man to get up and walk.
And the man did!
He was well!
Jesus had made him well!
Jesus loved the sick man and his four friends.

O ne day Jesus and His helpers went to Nain.
They saw people coming out of the city.
They were carrying the body of a young man
    who had died.
The young man's mother and the people were
    crying. Now she had no family.
Do you know what Jesus did?

TURN THE PAGE ▶▶▶

Jesus was sorry for the woman.
He made her son live again!
The mother hugged her son.
How happy she was.
Jesus loved the woman and her son.

Some children wanted to see Jesus.
They ran to meet Him.
Jesus' helpers said, "Jesus is busy. Do not
    bother Him."
Do you know what Jesus did?

TURN THE PAGE ▷▷▷

AND SEE

Jesus said, "Let the children come to me."
Jesus talked to the boys and girls.
Jesus listened to the boys and girls.
He had time for the children.
Jesus loved the children.

Jesus walked along a road.
A man was sitting beside the road.
The man could not see. He was blind.
He heard that Jesus was walking by.
He called out to Jesus.
He asked Jesus to make him see.
Do you know what happened?

TURN THE PAGE ▶▶▶

AND SEE

Jesus made the blind man see!
The man could see people and trees, grass
    and flowers, and the blue sky!
How happy the man was!
He thanked God.
Jesus loved the man who could not see.

Ten men had sores on their bodies.
The men were called lepers.
They saw Jesus walking by.
"Jesus, help us!" they said.
Do you know what Jesus did?

TURN THE PAGE >>>

AND SEE

Jesus spoke to the men.
The men looked at their arms and hands.
The sores were gone!
The men were well! Jesus had made them
    well!
Jesus loved the ten lepers.

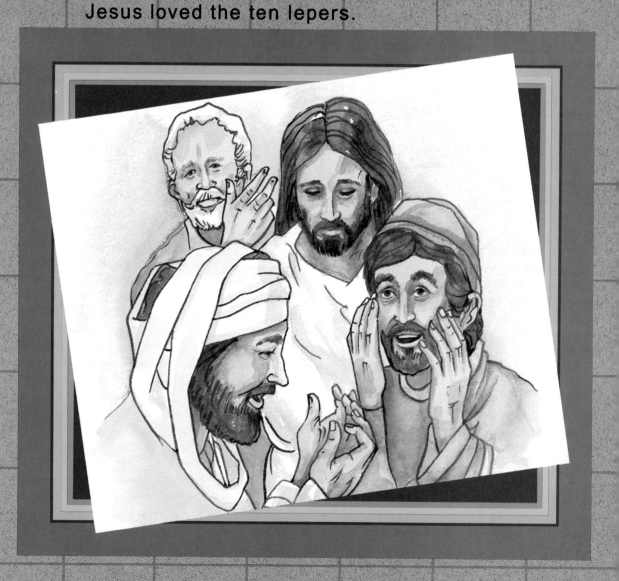

Mary and Martha cried and cried.
Their brother Lazarus was dead.
When Jesus saw how sad they were,
     He cried, too.
Do you know what Jesus did then?

TURN THE PAGE ▶▶▶

AND SEE

Jesus felt sorry for Mary and Martha.
He said, "Lazarus, come out."
Lazarus came out of the tomb!
He was alive! Jesus had made him live again!
Jesus loved Mary and Martha and Lazarus.

Jesus told a story about a shepherd.
A shepherd is a man who takes care of sheep.
The shepherd had one hundred sheep.
One sheep was lost.
Do you know what that shepherd did?

TURN THE PAGE ▶▶▶

AND SEE

The shepherd went out into the cold, dark
night.
He walked and walked. He called and called.
At last he found the lost sheep.
He took it in his arms and carried it home.
Jesus loves us as much as the shepherd loved
his sheep.

Jesus died for the sins of all the people of the
world.
He loved you and me enough to die for us.
This is the greatest love anyone ever had.
Do you know what happened after Jesus died?

TURN THE PAGE ▷▷▷

AND SEE

On the third day Jesus rose from the dead!
Jesus was alive!
Jesus died and rose again because He loves us.

J esus loves each person.
Jesus loves you.
He cares about you.
He will take care of you and help you.
Do you know how you can thank Jesus for His
   love?

TURN THE PAGE ▷ ▷ ▷

You can pray, "Thank You, God, for Jesus' love."
You can help others.
You can do things that please Jesus.
You can tell others about Jesus and His love.